SUPER

by

Jim Wortham

**LOVE STREET BOOKS**
P.O. Box 58163
Louisville, Kentucky 40258

**PRINTINGS**

First Printing     September 1975

Cover designed by Gail Sims

Published by:

LOVE STREET BOOKS
P.O. Box 58163
Louisville, Kentucky 40258

ISBN 0-915216-03-5
Library of Congress Catalog Card Number: 75-25329

Copyright © 1975 by Jim Wortham
Printed in the United States of America

**DEDICATION**

To all
who color
my world
with
    love
    and
    gentleness.

## OPEN ME

This book
is a theater.
Open these pages
with joyful expectation.

You will see me,
and my friends,
and my ways.

This theater
is a mirror.
If you look long enough,
you will see
        hear
        and touch yourself.

## YOU ARE SO BEAUTIFUL

You are one of those
beautiful people
who, when I see you,
I smile
and feel happy inside.

## FIRST MEETING

My hand
reaches for
your hand —
you accept
my touch.

I speak
of love —
you respond.

It seems
that we
have known
each other
forever.

## GYPSY

Gypsy girl,
your mysterious aura
makes you exotic.
Men are afraid
to ask you for a date.
They think you
will say, "No."

Gypsy girl,
your beauty
keeps you lonely.

## YOU ARE GONE

You spoke
of
love

and I
believed
you.

Now
you
are gone.

This
is how
it always is.

## AN ENDLESS DAY

When I am with you
it is like
a magic day
without beginning
or end.

## TRAPPED IN A BOX

I keep souvenirs
of our dates
in a box:

concert ticket stubs,
dried roses,
napkins,
shell earrings,
and love letters.

Daily I look through my box
dreaming of good times past.
But I find life's meaning
is slowly fading
now that you are gone.

My life
is trapped
in a box.

## MOVIE, DINNER & YOU

Was it the movie
that made me happy?

Or was it
the dinner?

Neither.
It was you.

## FIRST WEEK

I was careful
not to speak too soon,
or touch too fast.
My thoughts said,
"Walk carefully!"

## NO ROMANCE

If our relationship
is not to evolve
beyond friendship,
I must accept this.

## PRETTY BUTTERFLIES

Once upon a time,
a pretty girl
in the park
painted lovely things
like giant butterflies,
    yellow roses,
    the sun,
    and moon.
She tried
to capture in symbolic form
a conception of love.

Encountering her,
I decided that
real love
(she and I)
could be better than
capturing abstract love.

So I asked her
for a walk in the park.
    We held hands.
    We laughed.
    We hugged.
This was the beginning
of love.

No longer does she need
to capture love
in those mysterious forms.
She now has real love
to experience
and paint.

Her paintings are becoming
more beautiful,
and her art seems
more real.

## COKE DATES

Too much money
is spent

impressing
a new girl.

Either she likes you
or she doesn't.

Money shouldn't enter in.
Coke dates can be nice.

## A POETESS I NEVER KNEW
## OR
## GOOD-NIGHT, POETESS

I read about you.
The pages draw me
into your world of love,
joy and excitement.

At night
I dream
about spending
a lifetime with you.

Sometime,
maybe tomorrow,
I must realize
that a dream
is only a dream.

I must realize, also,
that I will
only know you
by the pages in your book.

Good-night,
Poetess.

## YOU & I

I want to be with you often
but I have no money
to take you to movies
and fancy restaurants.
But I can bring you colorful flowers
from my yard.
And for dinner
I can offer you peanut butter
and grape jam sandwiches
and whatever you want to drink.
In the evenings
we can take long walks
through the park
and stop along the way
for words of love.
After the walks
we can return home
and discover more about each other
while talking by candle light.
And then
you will realize
exactly how special you are
to me.

## TRY TO UNDERSTAND

I like
    quiet times,
        not wild parties.

I like
    soft music,
        not blurring sounds.

I desire
    honesty,
        not games.

I desire
    warmth,
        not indifference.

Will you
    understand
        me?

**HINTS**

How could you dance
into my life
with hints of love,
and then leave,
never to come
before my eyes again?

## SORRY

I am sorry
I ignored
your silent
cries for help.

The busy
days of
school,
sports and
work
drowned your voice.

I neglected you,
my friend.
I am sorry.

## ONE MILKSHAKE, PLEASE

Two straws
and

one
milkshake

is
enough

for
lovers.

## BEING ME

I will not try
to impress you.

I believe
being natural
is a treasure.

Look at me.
You will find beauty.

## SO TIRED

I am
tired of
studying.

I need
to share
this night
with someone.

**TOMORROW**

I sit watching
the clock take me
closer to tomorrow.

Bad — because
I have many things
to do.

Good — because
there is so much
to enjoy.

## MOON POWER

The moon is his strength.
I have seen him
weak,
slumping from lack of sleep,
under-fed
and unloved.

Many times it wasn't so.
Recently I saw him
dancing on the beach
like a young boy.

Tonight he is crawling
to the surf.
He looks at the moon
and energy flows into his body.
His body strengthens.

What happens,
I don't know.
The moon is his strength.
One day he will be a legend.

## A POEM FOR ESTELLA

    Wherever you
    are

    remember,

    we loved
    one
    summer.

## PATHS

Your path
and mine
have never
crossed.

It is
now time
for us
to meet.

## LAST NIGHT'S DELIGHT

You came into my life
when I needed someone.
We sat, listened to records,
and talked.
I shared with you
some of my dreams.
As I listened to you
I found myself dreaming again.
I loved watching you smile
and listening to you laugh.
Sometimes I tried to imagine
what you were thinking.
As it became late and we had to part,
I saw in your eyes that we should be
together again.

## SOPHISTICATION

When I return to simplicity
and act on compulsion,
people say
I'm acting unsophisticated.

To be OK
means to be detached,
unemotional, and to
speak boldly of freedom.

Don't return to simplicity, friend.
If you do,
you won't be OK.

## NUMBERS

Each phone number
I dial —

Busy . . .
No answer . . .
Sorry, she moved away . . .
Oh, she's married . . .
The number is now disconnected . . .

and the night goes on
in circles
of endless numbers.

I would talk to myself
but even my mind got up
and walked out of the room
to look for some activity.

## DREAMS

People say
you are living in a dream world.
You talk of
>being an actress
>writing a novel
>driving a jeep
>living on the beach.

No one listens.
They say you are dreaming.
They call you a child.

I will tell you
there is magic in the air!
Your dreams can come true.
If you need help,
someone will come running.

This is a beautiful world
for anyone who dares to dream.
Reach for those dreams today.
Someone will be there
to help you.

**WHEN IN LOVE**

When I am
in love,
everything about
life
falls into place.

When I
am not
in love,
nothing about
life
seems right.

# WALKING

I go out
and walk.

If anyone asks,
I will tell them,
"Sure I'm looking for someone
who might offer kindness."

No one asks that question.
No one is outside.

There is nobody to talk with.
There is nothing to do.
There is nothing else to be said.

## YES & NO

I change.
This is my right.

I am
the sum
of my experiences.

Today I
say yes
when yesterday
I said no.

Today I
say no
when yesterday
I said yes.

This is my right.
I change.

**MEMORIES**

When you are away
I close my eyes,
recall our yesterdays
and

    touch

        your

            hand.

## THE TEMPLE

Lady
at the temple,
I adore you.

When you smile,
love flows
from your presence.

I watch
as you
pray.

Beautiful lady,
touch me
with your peace.

## THE NIGHT THE LAUGHTER DIED

It happened one Friday night
at the Pizza Hut.
Shapely girls with their
      long hair
      and faded jeans
came to meet the guys
after the football game.

One football player bragged about sex.
Another told about a car he had stolen.
They all told their stories,
and they all laughed.

A football quaterback named Bill
had something different to say:
"I used to be on drugs.
I had sex with anyone I wanted.
I did anything for an ego trip."

(The air got heavy.
There was no plastic in Bill's voice.
Everyone knew he was telling the truth.)

Bill kept talking:
"Jesus gave me peace.
I don't need all those things anymore."

(You would expect a chuckle from someone.
But there was none.
All eyes were fastened on Bill as he talked on:)

"Now I have continuous joy
since I asked Jesus into my life."
Bill said no more.
He only looked down at the floor.

One by one,
the teenagers closed their eyes
in silent meditation.
One by one,
they found they needed only Jesus
to satisfy their longings in life.
I was there.
I know.

## MASKS

Your mask is hiding
a real person.
One who
    dreams
    loves
    and hurts.
You hope
someone
will accept
and love you.
Only then
will you be able
to take off your mask.

## MY RESPONSE TO MASKS

It's OK to wear masks.
Otherwise, cruel people
will hurt you.
Don't expose yourself
to everyone.
People don't know
how to react to a real person.
Walk carefully.

**LOVE CIRCLES**

I will love again
(I always do)

I will care again
(too soon)

And love will end again
(it always does)

**GO AWAY**

I tried
to forget
you.

Thoughts
invaded my
privacy

and
reminded
me.

## DISCOVERY

The problem
isn't
the inability
to communicate

but not
discovering ways

or perhaps
not wanting to.

## I CAN — YOU CAN

Poets and artists
are not the only people
who desire to be creative.
There is within each of us
the need to create something
that will bring joy to others.
Do not say
that you have no opportunities.
Begin where you are.
Use what you have
and you will attract
everything you need
to spread love
and beauty to others.

## VACATION ROMANCES

I like vacation romances.
You meet.
You touch.
Inhibitions are
left at home.

Just the two of you,
sharing laughter
and carefree days.

Vacation romances
are short enough
to be perfect.

## TEA

Sipping
tea

is how we
spend tonight.

Free and
easy.

We like it
this way.

## YOU LEFT

When you discovered
I was a person
with imperfections
like yours

you became
disinterested
and left.

**SILENT WORDS**

When we first met,
could you read my mind
when I was thinking,
 "I love you?"

## A PERFECT DAY

The wind
loosens your hair
as it blows across your face.

You hum
sweetly
while we walk.

Time slows down
and
love encircles us.

## QUESTIONS NEED ANSWERS

The question is:
Where do I fit in?

Am I at the top
or the bottom
of your list?

Please give me
a special place
in your dreams.

## WITHOUT WARNING

You said something wrong.
Unnecessary? Yes.
But it was said.

Our relationship
    crumbled
    before
    our eyes
as tension
charged the air.

And in silence,
you
    and
        I
            walked away
in different directions.

## A TOUCH OF SILENCE

Silence is needed.
There is a special kind of love
that comes by
looking into each other's eyes
and touching hands.

**PARADISE**

My
paradise
is
found
wherever
you
happen
to be.

## THE LAST NIGHT

Our last night
together
is here.

I
won't
cry.

There will be
too much time
for crying
later.

## SINGLE LIVING

You say
the single life
is wonderful:

All that free love,
no responsibility, and
going wherever you desire!

If single living
is so great,
why do I hear you crying
when I pass
your apartment?

## SEARCH

I will search for love.
A voice deep inside
tells me
there is someone.

## EACH DAY

During
each minute
of the day
remember,
"You are loved."

## PRIVACY

I must go
but I will return.

I must be alone
at times.

Please don't
invade my privacy.

Aloneness
is a part
of me.

I will be back.

## LOVE STREET BOOKS

TOUCHING YOU   TOUCHING ME   ($1.95)
by Jim Wortham

LOVING YOU   ($1.95)
by Jim Wortham

WILDFLOWER . . . poems for Joy   ($1.95)
by Lee Pennington

A LOVE LETTER AND OTHER POEMS   ($1.00)
by Julie of Colorado Springs

ART PRINT
"Wildflower."   11 x 14 inches.   ($1.00)

The above may be ordered from the publisher.
Please add 25¢ postage per item.  Send to:

LOVE STREET BOOKS
P. O. Box 58163
Louisville, Kentucky 40258